VOICES OF
DOGTOWN

POEMS ARISING OUT OF A GHOST TOWN LANDSCAPE

VOICES OF
DOGTOWN

POEMS ARISING OUT OF A GHOST TOWN LANDSCAPE

JAMES R. SCRIMGEOUR

8/8/19

*For Cindy,
a good poet in her
own write! Enjoy your
trek over the dogtown terrain!
All Best,
Jim Scrimgeour*

IP

LOOM PRESS
2019
Lowell, Massachusetts
www.loompress.com

Voices of Dogtown: Poems Arising Out of a Ghost Town Landscape

Copyright © 2019 by James R. Scrimgeour

ISBN 978-0-931507-16-8

Printed in the U. S. A.
First Edition
Cover photograph by James R. Scrimgeour and Linda McMillan
Book design by Victoria Dalis
Printing: King Printing Co., Inc., Lowell, MA

Loom Press
P. O. Box 1394
Lowell, Massachusetts 01853
www.loompress.com

for Chrissy (as always)

Acknowledgments

Early versions of "Abram Wharf (1738 ca–1814)," "There is No Moss Growing," "Wharf Road," "Old Ruth," and "Ruth's Ledge" published in *Bent Pin Quarterly*, January 2008.

Thanks to the Connecticut State University System for grants which made possible much of my early Dogtown research, and to Brian Clements for his careful reading of an early version of this work.

My sincere gratitude to the courteous, knowledgeable staff of the Cape Ann Museum, the Sandy Bay Historical Society, the Rockport Public Library, and the Sawyer Free Library who went out of their way to assist me with my research.

Thanks to all the guides and friends who have accompanied me on my many walks through Dogtown, including, but not limited to, Lisa Bouchie, Bill Dennis, George Hoffman (whose scientific expertise proved extremely helpful), J.D. Scrimgeour, and Ted Tarr.

Special thanks to Xanthi Scrimgeour and Jamie Scrimgeour for their assistance with design.

And heartfelt thanks to Carl Carlsen for his perceptive, intelligent introduction, for his careful proofreading of the later versions of the manuscript, and for his faith in my work.

My deepest appreciation to J.D. Scrimgeour and Christine Xanthakos Scrimgeour for the hours they spent with this manuscript. The final manuscript is far richer as a result of their suggestions.

And, of course, there is my indebtedness to and appreciation of all the artists, historians, poets, and novelists who have also been bitten by the Dogtown bug.

Thanks to Thomas Dresser for permission to quote from his book, *Dogtown, A Village Lost in Time.*

Thanks to the Cape Ann Museum for permission to quote from Joseph Garland's *The Gloucester Guide: A Retrospective Ramble.*

For modern-era sources, the author obtained permission from authors and/or publishers when available to reprint extended excerpts in this creative work. For any source which we were unable to reach in a fair attempt, the current rights holder should contact the author and publisher concerning appropriate terms for permission. Please note that all profits from sales of this limited-edition publication will benefit a community charity.

Cover Photo: Irregular Heart-Shaped Stone Boat

drifting in Granny Day's swamp—half-in,
half-out of wispy fleece cloud reflections—
we can feel the pressure; we know how much
the heart would love to get away, but we

know also the weight of the past—we feel
the magnetic pull both ways, the attraction
and repulsion of quivering dark fingers, the
reflections of the encircling trees and shrubs—

stone heart boat sitting so still in the midst
of a pretty postcard picture of the quicksand
swamp where so many, so much livestock
died—heart boat feeling a magnetic pull

on all sides, carrying us into and out of
the depths—and not going anywhere.

Table of Contents

Hearing the Voices of Dogtown

Many years ago, when I began teaching English at North Shore Community College, then located in Beverly, my colleague, Gloucester resident John Nelson, told me about Dogtown, a ghost town located in the highland of Cape Ann Massachusetts, and in a quiet, careful way, he made it seem haunted, dangerous and mysterious. I didn't think much more about it until 2002, when I expanded my college-supported website, *The Poetry of Places in Essex County*, www.poetryofplaces.org, and decided to include Dogtown. My library research and on-site exploration led me to marvel at the history and legends of Dogtown, its appeal to artists of many stripes, and the way it exists today as, to me, a kind of theme park offering scavenger hunts for rocks emblazoned with the numbers of the "cellar holes" of people who lived there two centuries ago as well as boulders inscribed with aphorisms. But it's much more than that, as this groundbreaking collection of poems by James Scrimgeour reveals.

Dogtown has long provided inspiration for poets and fiction writers including early 20th century poet and playwright Percy MacKaye, who sought to create a poetic form of democratic drama for America, Gloucester's two epic poets, Charles Olson and Vincent Ferrini, and contemporary best-selling author Anita Diamant. A visit to Dogtown revitalized the work of the great American painter Marsden Hartley, as the two exhibits of his work by the Cape Ann Museum have shown. Until now, Elyssa East's *Dogtown: Death and Enchantment in a New England Ghost Town* has done the best job of weaving together the various threads that create the fabric of the experience of the place that is Dogtown, and now James Scrimgeour comes forward with the single imaginative artistic work about Dogtown that I've been waiting for.

xiii

While reading James Scrimgeour's collection of Dogtown poems, I am struck by the many voices I hear, or more precisely, the voices Scrimgeour enables me to hear. Marsden Hartley characterized Dogtown as a combination of Stonehenge and Easter Island, an apt analogy that makes me realize those places that fascinate us the most harbor voices that speak to us and tell us of the numinousity of those places, that is, what makes them supernatural and mysterious. The voices in these poems of Scrimgeour's bring Dogtown alive in a multi-dimensional way that comes as close, in my judgment, as anyone has come so far to capturing the complete essence of Dogtown. When I finish reading these poems, when I have heard all the voices they contain, I think of Dogtown as if it is a sentient, breathing organism, and I marvel at my appreciation and understanding not only of the experience of Dogtown in particular, but also of the experience of place in general.

I find it helpful to divide these Dogtown poems into eight groups, and the first eight poems, from "Dogtown" to "Generalizations from Artifacts" are about What's Left Behind. In "Dogtown," what's left behind are the insights of generations of writers fascinated by Dogtown, and in this first poem, Scrimgeour establishes his m.o. of inserting their voices throughout the collection and respectfully subordinating his own voice to theirs. The end of the poem, "O.K. We're off . . ." invites the reader to come along with Scrimgeour as the adventure of becoming acquainted with Dogtown begins. In this section the geology and boulders of Dogtown are introduced through a consideration of "The Glacier," which has left behind "a cold chill / that resides still in the heart / of Cape Ann," and the terminal moraine whose rocks "have arranged themselves in suggestive sentences." These rocks think, speak and even dream. Also, left behind are the artifacts of the long abandoned Dogtown settlement, which together with what can be called the literature of Dogtown, cause Scrimgeour to listen and to consider things very carefully. And the one

Dogtown voice left behind the poet hears most prominently and most imaginatively is that of the legendary Tammy Younger, "quite a character," to say the least. To her, in my reading of the poems in her voice, Scrimgeour is the "old geezer," and the personal interaction between the two helps establish and enhance the timelessness of the Dogtown cosmos.

The next seven poems, from "The Last Lesson" to the first "Thomasine (Tammy) Younger—continued" capture the poet's uncovering Dogtowners' Lessons Left Behind. On the macro level, the history of Dogtown, or more properly the Commons Settlement, illustrates Roger Babson's four stages of the business cycle: improvement, prosperity, decline and depression. On the smaller stages of Scrimgeour's explorations, the "Cellar Holes" left behind show there are "no straight lines / in nature." When Scrimgeour goes to Granny Day's Swamp and the site of James Merry's mortal fight with the bull, he is absorbed by the timelessness of these places and the lessons the people associated with them have left behind. I must mention that for me, an aging athlete trying to keep the Reaper at bay, the lesson of James Merry is the most poignant and sobering of all. And so I follow the example of James Scrimgeour, who wants readers of these poems, and by extension visitors to Dogtown, to hear the voices left behind by Dogtowners that speak of their lives' lessons.

The following seven poems, from "Peter's Pulpit" to "Whale's Jaw, 2012," focus on The Erratics, the unique monumental boulders and rock formations the glacier left behind. The most famous of Dogtown's erratics is Whale's Jaw, and Scrimgeour hears it speak of its use as a subject by Marsden Hartley and Charles Olson. Scrimgeour's search to find Whale's Jaw illustrates the challenge of finding things in Dogtown: cellar holes, all of Babson's boulders inscribed with "truths," the rocks commemorating Merry. And when Whale's Jaw is "Finally Found," it not only yields the lesson that reality often differs from expectation, but it also enables Scrimgeour to bond with Olson across time through the photographs his son takes of him. Finally, to me, the most important poem in this group is "Dolphin's Jaw." It is an erratic that Scrimgeour has "found" and named. It is alive to him, like other boulders left behind, and it provides a lesson that sometimes while looking for one thing, we may find something else of equal or greater value. It also seems that at this point in the sequence of poems, the poet has begun to know Dogtown well enough to name one of its physical features and adopt it as his own. The poem reminds me of swimming along the eastern shoreline of Walden Pond and naming some of its features: The Lizard, The Silverbush, The Love Knot, and in so doing, making that place my own.

The centrality of the experience of Walking Through Dogtown lies at the core of the next four poems, from "Stroll through Brier Swamp," an area near Whale's Jaw, to "Dogtown Square," an easily reached central location. Scrimgeour focuses on the flora of Dogtown while conducting a "nature walk" in Brier Swamp, pays strict attention to the physical features of the rocks on the Babson Boulder Walk and carefully observes how the trees and other characteristics of Dogtown Square differ from his expectation, all the while, hearing voices.

The Timelessness of the Dogtown Community drives Scrimgeour's imagination in the next six poems from "Esther Carter" to "Lightning-Struck Tree." In these poems, a twenty-first century sensibility reaches out to and is engaged by the communal aspects of Dogtown. We get a sense of what living in the Dogtown community was like, and as the centuries melt into one another we are invited to consider, for example, Jack Bishop Smith's opinion of Marsden Hartley and the Babson Boulder Trail. Most interestingly, Scrimgeour brings Henry David Thoreau into the Dogtown community and in so doing crosses the centuries to make Thoreau's observations cosmically relevant to the present-day reader in "Boulders and Nutshells." Then, fittingly, in Thoreau-like fashion, he observes an element of nature, the "Lightning-Struck Tree," which he also makes a part of the Dogtown community and, like Thoreau would, he humanizes it and derives a lesson from it.

The focus is on Abram Wharf in the next seven poems, from "Abram Wharf" to "Thomasine (Tammy) Younger—Continued." Wharf's life reflects the downward spiral of Dogtown from prosperity to doom, and in this sequence of poems, Scrimgeour leads us to the imagined site of his suicide, the cellar hole marking the site of his home, and the voices Scrimgeour hears project what made Abram Wharf so human, so deserving of our empathy and so touchable, even today. As Tammy Younger comments, ". . . fact is we're all stuck here in this terminal moraine—feelin' the same comfort, the same pain. . . ."

The following eleven poems, from "Black Neil (Cornelius Finson)" to "Sammy Stanley," provide Compassionate Views of Dogtown Outliers. As we read these poems, we feel sympathy for Dogtown residents too often seen only through the lens of their idiosyncrasies. Freed slave Black Neil, the last remaining Dogtowner, is not someone who is willing to live in a hole in the ground, but a person seeking the comfort of a home. Freed slave Old Ruth is not the cross-dressing John Woodman, but a person, who in her work and in her spirit, has an affinity for the rocks and boulders which are so essential to the landscape of Dogtown. Embedded within this section is a sequence of poems about John Morgan Stanwood, who, with Abram Wharf and Tammy Younger, completes the trio of Dogtowners who fascinate Scrimgeour most. All three figure in the Stanwood sequence, and through the imagined writings of Stanwood found in his "boo," Scrimgeour channels Stanwood's voice to humanize them all. Worth noting too is the way Tammy Younger's voice tells us

xvii

what others label witchcraft is her way of exerting power in the face of marginalization. That she has become "hateful an' bitter" is understood by the old geezer who comments at the close of the poem: ". . . —nothing makes you as bitter and as hateful as repression."

The final five poems represent Twenty-first Century Dogtown. Although the two paintings by Marsden Hartley that inspired the beautiful ekphrastic poems within "Marsden Harley (1877–1943)" were done in the 1930s, they were both part of the Cape Ann Museum's 2012 exhibition, "Marsden Hartley: Soliloquy in Dogtown." And by concluding his treatment of Hartley's painting, "The Old Bars, Dogtown" by stating, "we have to supply our own captions," Scrimgeour reiterates his recurrent invitation: You come too and listen to the voices you hear. The next to last poem, "Looking for the Site," is prompted by Scrimgeour's search for where the 1984 murder in Dogtown described in Elyssa East's 2009 book occurred. It incorporates voices, references the trio of Wharf, Younger and Stanwood and invites the reader along on another frustrating experience of being unable to find something searched for in Dogtown. In the book's concluding poem, we hear the voice of Tammy Younger speaking across the centuries from her grave. At the behest of the old geezer, she's "beginnin' to think about thinkin' kindly of others—" and as she does this and as the book ends we too are invited to think kindly, compassionately, humanistically, and empathetically about the legendary inhabitants of Dogtown.

In this collection of poems, we are invited to reach out and touch Marsden Hartley, Charles Olson and all the other writers and artists inspired by Dogtown. We are invited to reach across the centuries and make the lives of Dogtowners object lessons for our own lives. We are invited to appreciate the plants and flowers of Dogtown and to understand its geology as embodied by the terminal moraine, the rocks and the boulders, and the erratics. We are invited to receive the inscribed truths that Roger Babson sought to convey. We are invited to visit Dogtown, to walk around, to experience that place for ourselves in our own way, to hear voices and to be guided by the approach taken by James Scrimgeour in this transcendent collection of poems that will take its place as a culminating work within the literature of Dogtown.

—Carl Carlsen

Dogtown

"is delusion," (Garland, p.63)

is "the Rune of [Our] Nation" (Olson, p.508)
in which we can read our end,

is 3600 rock-strewn acres "located on high land.
It abounds in boulders, large and small.
In and near Dogtown are several swamps,
but otherwise the soil is gravelly and arid.

"It is a land where blueberries, huckleberries,
blackberries, bayberries, sweet fern, and red cedar
flourish. Many birds nest there in the summer; and
in the autumn, when the open areas are carpeted with
blue asters and the bushes are clothed in brilliant red
and purple, it is a popular . . . stop for great flocks of birds
migrating to the south." (Copeland and Rogers, pp.32-33)

"A few hours [in] Dogtown stumbling over
the stony paths, swatting mosquitoes, hearing
the winds rattle the dry brush, pondering
the pitiful cellar holes, wondering how anyone
could have lived in such a spooky place,
are enough to restore sociability." (Garland, p.57)

This "cluster of deserted houses, [was] too
difficult of access to remove even their materials,
so . . . they [were] left to moulder alone." (Higginson, p.254)

1

"The poor widows have all found rest in the grave;
and the old dwellings that scarcely afforded a shelter
for their declining years have also disappeared:
but the ancient cellars, the grass grown roads,
and the traditions of the place, still impart
a melancholy interest to the deserted hamlet." (J.J. Babson, p.450)

"For many, Dogtown Common conjure[s] up
legends, freaks, pranks, and witch scenes
of a Faustian nature." (Swan, p.139)

Dogtown Common is "an elevated table-land,
overspread with great boulders as with houses,
and encircled with a girdle of green woods and
an outer girdle of blue sea. I know of nothing
more wild than that gray waste of boulders;
it is a natural Salisbury Plain, of which icebergs
and ocean currents were the Druidic builders;
in that multitude of couchant monsters there seems
a sense of suspended life; you feel as if they must
speak and answer to each other in the silent nights,
but by day only the wandering sea birds seek them,
on their way across the Cape, and the sweet-bay
and green fern imbed them in a softer and
deeper setting as the years go by." (Higginson, pp.253-4)

"The deserted village is the excitement and thrill
of desolation and abandonment." (Mann, quoted by Dresser, p.3)

"The settlement at Dogtown was merely something
of an eddy in the . . . history of Cape Ann." (C&R, p.43)

"It is the lonely highland of Cape Ann,
empty of habitation, abandoned by the dogs
and even by the cows that used to find
thin pasture there, left to the ghosts
of its deserted village. It's where you're off to . . .
when the world is too much with you." (Garland, p.57)

O.K. We're off . . .

First Trip to Dogtown

Past the Cape Ann rifle and pistol range
and the steam rising off the compost heap—
turn right just before the dump and pass
the path to the spring that people still
go to for clear water—Sylvester Ahola,
trumpeteer, practiced here, the guide says—

the trail narrows, turns—we pick our way
downhill to the reservoir made from damming
Alewife Brook—a foggy mist rises off the water—
we see distorted, rippling reflections
of deciduous trees—rounded dark
forest-green forms in the grey water.

We walk along to the far end—where
looking back the long way, three wraiths
of mist shroud the distant shore—we see
clearly only what is directly before us—

orange rocks that have arranged themselves
into suggestive sentences
on the corrugated grey slate.

Thomasine (Tammy) Younger (1753–1829)—Introduction

the "Queen of the Witches"—lived in the Fox Hill Homestead,
on the outskirts of Dogtown, on a hill that is now Cherry Street. . . .

It's gettin' close to closin' time—nothin' here but those
f…in' arseholes on their dirt bikes—more and more of them—
gunnin' past—those damned fat tires squealin' over and over—
been what-is-it seventy, eighty years now since a soul
who understood anythin' at all came by to visit—

not since that painter Hartley Marsden or Marsden
Hartley, whatever his name was, a bit of a fool
in any case, but he understood some things, he felt
the sadness that has seeped into the rocks—connected
he was, tied to the boulders as surely as that clown,
Stanwood, old Abram an' I have been—But Hartley,
artist an' all, used the grotesque energy of the place—
freed his spirit by painting the ghosts he saw in the rocks
that held him—an option closed to lost, wanderin' spirits
without hands of flesh and blood. . . .
                                  Oh, look
at this old decrepit geezer who just came in—
moving kinda slow with his arthritic joints (I know
what that's like) and carryin' his notebook and camera—
I try to despise him like I do all the others, but I can't,
at least not as much—he senses we're here, and he seems
to care about us, about the unholy trinity of doomed souls
hauntin' this boulder-strewn God-forsaken landscape
fer close ta two hundred years.

Yep, fer sure, he sees the three
Abram, Captain Jack and me—does he think
he can free his spirit by painting us—I wonder . . . strange,

f...in' weird how I see so clearly into and through him,
an' he sees into and through me—hafta admit it's kinda nice
to finally have someone tell our story from my point a view—
tho I wish he wouldn't clean up my language so much—
all those f...in' dots—aaarrrgggh!!! Whassee wanna do—
sell his book in the tourist shops—hmmmmm, might do
the tourists some good to read somethin' a little nearer
the truth—an' the geezer has an edge I kinda like . . .

The Glacier

We can barely sense
the enormous pressure

in the immense depths of the towering
ice-mountain that in its slow grinding

journey over the surface of the earth
ingested more of the beauty and more

of the terror of the natural world
than we can possibly imagine,

transformed these minor irritants into
grotesque semi-precious stone-poems,

and then excreted them as it retreated
back to its home in the north leaving

a terminal moraine, and a cold chill
that resides still in the heart

of Cape Ann.

In the Moraine, Dogtown Common, Cape Ann, 1931
(Oil on academy board)—after the painting
by Marsden Hartley (Cape Ann Museum, p.27)

Thin white fish clouds swimming in light blue sky
above the cluster of rocks—grey, cream, beige
and other earth tones—
                                two boulders stand out,
rising out of a bed of dark shrubs—towering over
the broken, discarded skulls of others . . .

one, an angular flat-topped intellectual rock
with four rusty bloodshot eyes—(from drinking
too much, or thinking too hard, perhaps)—

two eyes above and two below the diagonal
straight line mouth that appears to be a slight
ironic smile—no matter whether it is upside

down, no matter which pair of eyes it goes with—
all four eyes are open, all four are staring—not
at the wriggling eely clouds, but at something
beyond the frame . . .
                           the other boulder,
the more sensuous one with dark grass
sideburns, bald right forehead, curved black
shadow mouth, eyes closed, more rounded
human head in repose—dreaming . . .

A Community of Boulders

large and small, beige and grey houses
deposited centuries ago by a retreating
glacier—homes, rounded and smooth—

no doors, front or back—cracks for
windows, rare bluebirds resting on or
beneath the eaves—wild shrub hedges

here and there, bayberry bushes imported
by the colonists—with thorns and clusters
of shiny red tear-shaped berries—guarding

the non-existent doors—and other assorted
bushes of berries: huckle, blue, and black
growing improbably out of rock-strewn lawns,

lit now in autumn with patches of color:
blue asters, sweet ferns, and the familiar
flaming red sumac—color seasoning

sprinkled around and over the ever-baked,
ever-standing rocks by a stagnant swamp
quicksand pasture—see how the rust-colored

Alewife Brook winds serpentine amongst
these homes that lie as if they had rained
down on the landscape—these ancients

with cells that never sleep, living molecules
of thought and feeling stirring within—
cells always tingling as other life forms

clamber over and around, live and die
amongst them—this community speaks
to us of the pain of all those unable to die,

speaks to all mortals in bitter,
in sweet unheard tones.

Tabulation of Artifacts

from "unknown" cellar site:

redware (inexpensive and utilitarian
pottery made locally from clay
that turned red upon firing)
12 unglazed—23 brown glaze—
12 black glaze—other colors (red,
green and brownish-yellow)—3

other ceramics: delftware—18
salt-glazed stoneware—6
creamware—75 porcelain—3

window and bottle glass: green bottle
glass—13 green window glass—5
flip glass—6 (from English tumblers)

nails and iron—16

pipe stems and bowls: stems—25
bowls—9

animal bones and teeth: bones—12
teeth—1

miscellaneous: one rectangular
iron plate (2.5 x .75 inches)
one iron oxen shoe fragment
2.75 inches long (Sucholeiki, pp.16-17)

fragments—only fragments . . .

but "photographing and documenting some of these artifacts
should go along [sic] way in demystifying these people,
as well as to give us some insight into their daily lives."
(Sucholeiki, p.1)

Generalizations from Artifacts

The residents of Dogtown owned
a lot of pottery, had a few shillings
to buy English ceramics, smoked tobacco,
had at least one flintlock firearm, sheep,
goats and at least one horse.

Their clothes utilized copper alloy
buckles and buttons;

they were poor without doubt.

All store ledgers, ship cargo logs
and tax records show that the Days
(e.g.) never purchased anything.

Artifacts from the cellars of both
Granny Day and Unknown are similar
and confirm above. (Sucholeiki, p.43)

A true statement, but consider just a small
portion of what we are about to encounter:

rocks with mottoes or "1st attacked" carved
into them—the rock creatures in Boulder Pond—
the rock, under which we can imagine old
Abram Wharf died—Elyssa East's book detailing
the death of Anne Natti, a teacher of special ed—
the Dogtown rock that bashed in her head . . .

consider also Dresser's chapbook—the works
of Garland, Mann, Copeland, Rogers, and all
the other historians—Higginson's reminiscences—
Blessington and Diamant's novels—the relevant
Olson poems—Hartley's poems and paintings—
photos of Whale's Jaw, past and present—the entry
in Thoreau's journal—this poem—this sequence
of poems. . . .

Are any of these artifacts?
How are they similar? How different?
What generalizations can we draw from them?
What above do they, can they confirm?

The Last Lesson

Jane "Granny" Day (1720–1814),
the school mistress of the single-room
schoolhouse just across Wharf Road
from her home "considered herself
quite a competent school teacher, though
the competition was somewhat slim." (Dresser, p.17)

In back of the schoolhouse was
Granny Day's Swamp, "a stagnant bog,
dank, dark and dire" (Garland, p.65)
where livestock sometimes became mired—

many sheep, cattle, and horses occasionally
wandered in, and got "bogged down . . .
like the mastodons, for keeps." (Garland, p.65)

Her last lesson: for all who follow her—
keep open a watchful eye, lest we, like
the unfortunate livestock, like Granny Day,
become mired in a bog that bears our name—

for keeps.

On a Rock in Granny Day's Swamp

a full professor, his L.L. Bean slacks
torn by thorns, sits thinking of students,
his students, and Granny Day's—over

200 years ago: Judy Rhines, Molly Jacobs,
Sarah Phipps, Jack Bishop Smith, Oliver
Younger, Johnny Morgan Stanwood,

et al., wondering if she lived to see
the twisted, gnarled, stunted growth. . . .
The professor looks over the line of rushes,

sphagnum moss, and cinnamon fern
at the edge of Boulder Pond, and wonders
what will he live to see; he looks at

the boulders, themselves, that dominate
the scene; he sees the same half-submerged
rock creatures, basking without lotion,

without motion in the same sun,
thinner ozone layer, but the same sun
as two hundred years ago. Are those

the same large black birds twittering
in the undergrowth? Is it the same
quicksand beneath our feet?

Granny Day's Swamp, Revisited

Now, here we are again on the left side
of Wharf Road poking around in the swampy
area behind what was, two hundred years ago,

her schoolhouse—we make our way through
a criss-crossed network of brambles and branches,
stepping only on rocks and firm ground,

not wanting to add our bones to those of the cows
and sheep that wandered into this "slough of despond" (Garland, p.65)
and never walked out—we peer through a small

leaf and thorn-fringed opening in the undergrowth
at a black pool with small grey-purple face-sized
patches of scum (insect eggs perhaps) floating on it,

shimmering faces, ghosts from the past—their sad
off-white feline eyes looking up and out at our own
war-torn, religion-addled twenty-first century—

look there, see the quicksilver tears trickling down
their cheeks—see the tears, tears, and more tears
of all the trapped creatures that never get out—

and the tears for all the trapped creatures
who think they do.

The Desertion of the Village

known as Dogtown, due primarily to economics,
no doubt, but "greatly accelerated by the enormous
drain of the male members of that section who shipped
aboard the privateers, [during the Revolutionary War]
losing their lives beneath the waves or in prisons,
leaving mothers, wives, children and the aged
in dire destitution to eke out an existence
as best they could." (Pringle, p.83)
                                        "There were living,
[in Dogtown] twenty years after the war, sixty
of this unfortunate class [war widows] . . . and the last
of them are still remembered, as they were seen
bearing to market the berries and herbs
which yielded them a scanty support." (J.J. Babson, p.450)

The process of desolation and degradation accelerated rapidly
as most of the remaining males moved to the coastal communities,
or committed suicide.
                                "The deserted dwellings,
the half-filled cellars marking their site, perpetuate
a mournfully pathetic tale to those who follow local annals
and recall vividly the sufferings entailed on the innocent
by the operations of war." (Pringle, p.83)

"I kinda like the way he said that."—a silky voice
echoes in my inner ear.

Cellar Holes

once square—now oval,
once solid foundations tumbling
inward to the center—

no straight lines
in nature.

Wrestling the Bull

James Merry, a Gloucester young man,
the story goes, (Copeland and Rogers, pp.36-37)
shipped out as a seaman on a vessel

which brought salt from the Mediterranean.
He visited Spain, witnessed several bullfights
and met some of the toreadors. After his return

his talk was all bull and bullfighting—friends
suggested he show them how it was done,
and he began to wrestle with a young bull calf

pastured at Dogtown. Since Merry was six-foot-
seven and weighed over two-hundred-fifty pounds,
he threw the bull easily enough and began

staging exhibitions of bullfighting for his friends.
Next year, however, the bull was much heavier
and stronger, and in his first exhibition, after

a long struggle, Merry went limp from exhaustion
and had to be rescued by the spectators. Weeks later
[September 10, 1892—to be exact]—challenged

perhaps by the feat of a man who had thrown a calf
by the tail over Squam Bridge—he went out alone
one morning (blueberrying, he told his wife),

left his pail at the edge of the pasture and
stepped inside for a private match with the bull.
Late that afternoon, when he had not returned,

neighbors went to search for him and found
his body. The trampled grass and bloody rocks
showed that Merry had been thrown many times

against the boulders. The bull, with blood
on his horns, was feeding calmly nearby. . . .
Interesting story—even though Merry shipped out

as a "young man" and was over 60 when
he went out into the Dogtown pasture for his
final session with the bull. . . . Three boulders

with barely legible runes ("1st attacked,"
"2nd attacked" etc.) mark the scene of the fight—
three boulders—in a field—the blood washed

and not washed away—three boulders—
so smooth and so cold—today,
when I touch them.

Thomasine (Tammy) Younger—Continued

ya, the geezer has a artist's touch, a edge,
like Hartley, like that Thoreau character who came by—
just one night wendin' his way slowly through the shadows
of the rocks, jottin' notes in his journal—ya, he had his edge—
he knew some things the good townspeople don't—he knew
how the poor suffer when f...in' presidents
or would-be presidents start their wars—

an he knew what it's like to live alone—I jus'
don' understand why it never bothered him, to live,
like me, alone, mocked and despised by the reverends,
bankers, and tradesmen that call theirselves the world. . . .
Aarrggh!!! It enough to make you gag—the villagers,
they can't despise me any more than I despise them. . . .

Aah! the sneers, the insults of those who mocked me
when they dared, but not to my face—I still laugh
when I think of that fool who knocked the pumpkins
from my porch, my fall harvest rollin' down the hill
into the creek—that arsehole spent one entire hot
Indian summer afternoon carryin' pumpkin after pumpkin
up the hill and pilin' them up again on my porch—
he knew it was either that or else . . .
                                        he was afeard
I might turn him into a rabbit—a sheep, perhaps, so
his outsides would look like his insides—pugh!!!

22

Peter's Pulpit

huge die-shaped rock named for no reason
that anyone remembers—but could be
the rock on which Peter built his church—

a nearly inaccessible altar and whatever lives
within looks out through a trinity of dark bars—
green, brown and black, drawn on the near side

of the rock—lines of lichen and moss following
small run-off streams from cracks in the dome. . . .
In an extremely dry habitat—the biologist

explains—how long moisture lasts (i.e.,
how long we remain capable of tears)
determines what gets established.

Whale's Jaw

"After 300 yards it [Commons Road] swings north,
by a boulder called Peter's Pulpit for no . . . apparent reason,
and descends into the ghoulish greenery of Brier Swamp.
We have to keep an eye peeled for the left fork

"which is identified by a metal culvert crossing the path. . . .
A short way on, and back up into the pasture and the sunlight,
and there is Whale's Jaw, a most memorable rock split agape
eons ago by frost or lightning. Yes, with some imaginative effort

"to be sure, it's a breeching Moby Dick about to clamp with an
earthshaking snap on the leg of Captain Ahab. If we're young
and springy and well-sneakered, we scramble to the lip
of the greater mandible, where a grand view

"should be the prize."(Garland, p.66)

Dolphin's Jaw

definitely not a whale we found
on an off trail while searching for

Whale's Jaw—still, interesting in
its own right—as I clamber down

from its modest peak and look back
wondering—is there some reason

we were led astray? I must admit
there is some grandeur in this strange

rock spotted with brown lichen (much
as his sea cousins are speckled with

barnacles)—grandeur in this diseased,
cracked and broken stone with snout

raised and sniffing the salad greens
with red berries hovering before

his half-open mouth.

Study for Whale's Jaw, Dogtown
(after the drawing by Marsden Hartley)

who first visited Dogtown in 1920—and devoted
spring and summer of 1931 to capturing Dogtown
in poems and paintings—"It is said that Hartley
recovered his artistic direction during
his Dogtown interval." (Dresser, p.23)

See, for example, his *Study for Whale's Jaw*
hanging in the Cape Ann Museum—stark
black and white, the larger

upper jaw appears as a shadow
of a man, a short, prosperous rotund

man squatting, toad-like, looking
into the lower jaw, into his own

shroud-draped coffin.

Charles Olson

saw Dogtown as "the Rune of Our Nation"
in which we can read our end

see letter #7 of "Maximus, to Gloucester"
for his take on Marsden Hartley

and his view of Whale's Jaw,
and the other strewn boulders—

the sensitive Hartley relieved
the starkness of the scene—he

put the softness, the human back
into it—after Nature (who knew

what she was about) had spent a
few hundred thousand years taking

it out—Olson contrasts the human
with the rock—instead of blending

them together—see the photo in
the Sawyer Library of O's father

inside the jaw (shades of James Merry)—
as if his puny human strength were

forcing the jaw apart.

Finally Found

Lo and behold! The long sought after Whale's Jaw—
but different from the book—this large lump of rock
decorated with spray-painted graffiti now serves as
a public square in the wilderness where the weary
traveler can rest and watch the "parade of joggers,
hikers, dogs and their walkers, berry-pickers, [and]
lovers" (Pope, p.74) that is likely to wander by—

see the tourist trampled grass all around, and
the lower jaw split off from the upper, the dark
coffin shape lying in shadow on the ground—

the result of some camper's fire, they say, but
I wonder—did Olson's father really weaken it . . .

yet it remains a huge mournful mammal—
rising grey out of woven green sea—suspended
in time as the line of sunlight so slowly
climbs and descends its granite flanks—

in the photo—I am not that young or springy,
but I am well-sneakered and standing atop
the head where a spout might be—
thinking of Olson,
                            of human contrast
to the rock—just existing, just living in or
off nature is not enough, he says, he wants
new creation—new additions to the scene . . .

and looking down on well-trodden grass,
no ocean in sight, I admit he's got a point,
but to fix things, to remember, to restore,
to bring the dead back to life is O.K. too,

I add, while looking over a moraine
of boulders, some red cedar trees, and
my son with a camera pointing at me.

Whale's Jaw, 2012

no longer a whale,
but a toad—

squatting on haunches
in a patch of sun—

the burnt-out taste
of human campfires

and its unnecessary
tongue spit out,

lying there, lying where
and how it fell.

Stroll through Brier Swamp

pleasant enough coming or going through
the no longer ghoulish greenery, we can
stroll past the tree with a blue dot to mark

the trail and a very neat band of horizontal
holes—the work of the yellow-bellied
sap-sucker, (a sophisticated woodpecker

who eats no trash, dines only on the sweetest
fare); let's take our own sweet time, as we
look for rare plants like buckbean, sundew,

the carnivorous pitcher plant, and the many
varieties of orchid: Arethusa, Calopogon,
Pagonia, flowers so beautiful, flowers

so very rare—finding only the pitcher plant, but
"That's O.K.," the silky voice out of everywhere
whispers, "Imagined blooms are sweeter."

The Mottoes

"I [was] really trying to write a simple book with words
carved in stone instead of printed on paper."
(Roger Babson, quoted by Dresser, p.23)

"An intervention of the worst sort
it seems to me." (Marsden Hartley, quoted by Oaks, p.10)

But, at least, it gave some work to quarry workers—who
(with bad timing) went out on strike one week before
the stock market crash and were never rehired.

"In the vicinity of Dogtown Square and along the path
to Gloucester are some of the most picturesque boulders
in Dogtown. On the faces of several of them mottoes
were carved . . . [in the 1930's] at the instance [sic] of
Roger W. Babson, the well-known native of Gloucester.

"The letters in the mottoes are ten inches tall and . . .
carved with expert workmanship. . . . The boulders
on which the mottoes were carved are located on a tract
of eleven hundred acres which Mr. Babson gave to the city
of Gloucester in the watershed of the Babson Reservoir.

"By the terms of the gift the tract is always to be kept
as a public park for the use of all the inhabitants
of Cape Ann." (C&R, p.38) The following are

examples from his book of stones:

IDEALS   SAVE   HELP MOTHER
GET A JOB   KEEP OUT OF DEBT

PROSPERITY FOLLOWS SERVICE and
NEVER TRY NEVER WIN

this last near the field
where Merry died.

Babson Boulder Walk (2005)

I

From his reservoir, we turn back uphill,
run smack into TRUTH—a single word,
ten-inch letters carved into a large
flat-faced stone and painted black—

would that it were always
that easy to see.

II

TRUTH, the first page in
the prohibitionist's most

lasting work—carved with
expert workmanship by

unemployed stone cutters
during the Depression.

III

Then COURAGE in the same expert hand,
the same large letters, the same black
paint with a smaller skull-shaped rock
covered with mold and balanced
precariously on top.

IV

On LOYALTY, lichen and algae
live together in a symbiotic relationship—

the lichen, a pale green fungus
clings tightly to the rock
and provides a frame house

for the algae which, in turn,
provide food and nourishment
for the house, for the security
in which they live.

V

Walking all the while over
twisted roots—encountering

IDEAS and INDUSTRY—two rocks
close together—if not in our century,

then at least in Babson's head.

VI

IF WORK STOPS VALUES DECAY

tucked away on a side trail next
to cellar hole #22—once the home
of Joseph Riggs, son of Andrew—
#22 chosen simply because

the slight indentation is still here—
in this place—at this time.

VII

While just past KINDNESS
we come across an example
of "inclusion," a piece

of granite that fell into
the magma of colliding
tectonic plates—still

stuck, still resting there
thousands of years later—

clearly an example
of INTEGRITY.

VIII

Another side trip to
the only rock with words
carved into both sides—STUDY

on one side and BE ON TIME
on the other.
                (Was it Babson
or the stone cutter who
decided on this pairing?

Was Granny Day consulted?)

IX

But the most interesting, most
imposing rock on the trail split
straight down the middle by lightning
perhaps or by some plant or plants
growing in a small fissure:

SPIRITUAL POWER on the left side—
the right just ignorant blank stone—

I have my picture taken in front of
this split stone—thinking of the political
symbolism, thinking maybe
it will seep in.
                    "But,
in the picture," the silky voice asks,
"Won't everything be reversed?"

Dogtown Square

"The air of obstinance and delusion, of pathos
and tragicomedy amidst grim subsistence which
surrounded the decay of Dogtown seems to hang
heaviest as we approach the crossroad
of Dogtown Square." (Garland, p.65) Now,

in a new millennium, it's hard to imagine
this land without trees, but easy to feel
the glacial chill that darkens our view
of the bright sunlit scene; look, for example,

at my photograph—hard to imagine this
intersection of paths euphemistically called roads
being the center of anything, certainly not
a thriving settlement of over seventy families—

but easy to feel the desolation—see how
the thin straight trunks of young trees with
their tops cropped rise like Monet's Poplars
to the left or right of the trail to or from

the reservoir—see the serpentine sunlit path
either lifting up or sprouting from the small
grey boulder partially covered by leaves and
vines—a boulder with the marking "D.T.Sq."

firmly chiseled and neatly painted black. It's
a place "to strip the soul into its wild admissions"
Olson said, (p.384) "wild," well, later maybe—

but all the souls we've met so far—whether
looking right or left, inward or outward,
forward or back—admit only the chosen few,

a few carefully chosen words.

Esther Carter (1755 ca–1836)

Her family is supposed to have come from England
in 1741. Kind, hospitable, and widely known, she
lived a poor but selfless existence. Her door

was always open to visitors, and she would share
what meager fare she had with them. Boiled cabbage
was her best known offering. Other poor would gather

berries, but she had her pride. "I eats no trash," she said.
(C&R, p.33) She lived off the land with her cattle,
sheep, and team of oxen.

She was a spinster who went out nursing, and "Her house
had no cellar—only a potato pit, but it was the only
two-story house in Dogtown," (Dresser, p.16) "and it
was clapboarded, the clapboards being fastened with
wooden pegs.
            "After she moved to the village
at the harbor, her dwelling continued to be known as
'the [Esther] Carter house.'" (C&R, p.35)

"Her home became a popular picnic site long after she
was no longer around to offer a meal to passersby." (Dresser, p.16)
She died, living with friends on School Street in Gloucester

"amidst unaccustomed luxury . . . killed by Kindness,"
Groom wrote. (p.2) Since she died in 1836 and Black Neil
(the last living resident of Dogtown) was taken to

the poorhouse in 1830 and since people had been
using her house for many years after she left,
she had, it appears, sufficient time to become

accustomed to luxury and was probably killed
by a more natural cause than kindness.

Becky (Granny) Rich

"gained a reputation telling fortunes
from coffee grounds. Her fortunes were always
cheerful and optimistic, if not always reliable.

"She was known for concocting witch-like brews
from native berries.
                          "Becky [like Esther Carter]
was reputed to boil cabbage dinners for the local youth
and lead a merry life for all she came in contact with.

"Her son, [grandson?] Jack Bishop Smith, was one of two
Dogtown residents known to have committed suicide."
(Dresser, p.16)

"One cheerful vision too many,"
a new voice, a raspy one echoes
also in the inner ear.

Unanswered Questions about Jack Bishop Smith

How old was he when he died? Was he the son or
the grandson of Becky Rich? What kind of student
was he at Granny Day's? How did he get along
with Becky? With Rachael? Did he ever drink

any of their concoctions? Did he have any lovers?
Any friends? What did he think of Abram Wharf?
Tammy Younger? Captain Jack Stanwood?
Judy Rhines? Black Neil? Old Ruth? or any other

Dogtowner? What does he think of Babson's
Boulder Trail? Of Marsden Hartley? How connected
was Smith to the Dogtown terrain? In what landscape
is his sorry misbegotten soul wandering now?

"I'd like to know that, myself!"
ol' raspy voice chimes in.

Aunt Rachael

"Every year at vernal fever time," Rachael Smith,
daughter of Becky (Granny) Rich and mother (maybe)
of Jack Bishop Smith, "would mix her mystic concoction
of foxberry leaves, spruce tops and suchlike greeneries,
and descend into town to peddle this brew from door
to door. 'Now Ducky,' [she] would cackle to the lady
of the house, 'I've come down to bring a dire drink,
for I know you feel springish.'" (Garland, p.57)

"When their house became too dilapidated for habitation,
Becky and Rachael moved into [Esther] Carter's home
which soon developed a reputation as a 'road house'
promoting dancing and other frivolity for the youth
of the area." (Dresser, p.16)
                          Rachael once held
a "wall paper party," each guest brought scraps
of paper and they "did" the house,
"the harlequin effect being quite pleasing
to her, apparently." (Mann, p.41)

She often entertained parties of young people
from Riverdale and Annisquam, and she, like Esther
and Becky, boiled cabbage, baked Johnnycakes,
told fortunes from coffee grounds, and generally
helped the youth to have a good time.

"The [Esther] Carter house was 'somewhere to go'
for the young people of the neighboring villages
[in the early 1800's], and it is easy to imagine

that the spectral shadows of the boulders and cedars
along the Dogtown paths gave a romantic setting
for such excursions, especially on the long walks
home in the moonlight." (C&R, pp.35-6)

Boulders and Nutshells

In September 1858, walking through the same
romantic setting, the same spectral shadows,
Thoreau saw no lovers; he saw only the "hills

"strewn with boulders, as though they had rained
down, on every side. . . . When the moon rose,
what had appeared like immense boulders

"half a mile off in the horizon now looked
by contrast no larger than nutshells or
burlnut against the moon's disk, and she

"was the biggest boulder of all." (Thoreau,
quoted by Dresser, p.20)—so in the journal,
the lovers' moon turns into a boulder—the lovers'

boulders into nutshells—and here, in this poem,
the lovers themselves, freed from their
discarded husks, turn into charged particles

of soul-stuff, cling to whoever chooses
to tell of or listen to them.

Lightning-Struck Tree

A current Dogtown resident, lying
with dead and dying limbs branching
upward and outward in all directions;
trunk splintered—its stump

looks like a wild white flower
blooming beside the upright tree
next door—the upright neighbor
that holds three stricken limbs

of the fallen tree in a "V" about
10 feet off the ground—three limbs—
each with a splintered end—three
orphaned mini-flowers—lost souls

rooted in thin air—their stems
pinned in the neighbor's crotch—
a strange bouquet of still flowering
green leaves—see what one living thing

may salvage from the fall of another.

Abram Wharf (1738 ca–1814)

is "listed in the Massachusetts Tax Assessment
of 1771 as owning one house, a head of cattle,
one swine and 3 acres of pasture land with
an annual worth of 2 pounds, 2 shillings" (Sucholeiki, p.49)

the most educated man in Dogtown, a cousin
of Theophilus Parsons, Chief Justice of the Massachusetts
Supreme Court—respectable Abram played by the rules,
lived in Dogtown all his life—on February 9, 1762

(age 24) he married Mary Allen, daughter of Benjamin Allen
and Mary Riggs. By 1800 he had become a noted
shepherd and farmer and owned most of the sheep
in town. As he watched the decline of the village,

his own house became "hardly habitable"
and one day in 1814, Old Abram (aged 76 years)
"sat by the fire sharpening his razor.
                                        "'Sister,' said he,
'do you think people who commit suicide go to heaven?'

"'I don't know; but I hope you will never do such a thing, . . .'
was her answer. 'God forbid,' was his solemn response.

"Soon, he slipped the razor into his shoe, . . . went out," (Mann, p.54)
and "put [the] razor to his neck and crawl[ed] under a boulder
to die." (Dresser, p.15) Legend says no moss will ever grow
on that rock.

His estate: a dwelling house and land under
and adjoining: about two acres: $75.00; two acres of salt marsh,
more or less in Annis Squam river farm creek: $60.00; and
a wood lot: $20.00.
Debts: Coroner: $13.10; Physician: $12.84;
Funeral Charges and incidental expenses: $34.50. (Sucholeiki, p.49)

So, his life—what did it profit him?
Did he come out ahead?

"Whoa, Whoa,"

the raspy voice intones,
"don't forget the $116.20
owed for property tax in 1978," (East, p.201)

"and why don't they come out
to this God-forsaken place
and try to collect it?" he asks.

There is No Moss Growing

on either of the two rocks wedged
together to form a stone tent, just
a dead wishbone branch leaning

against the larger, the branch standing
on guard, half-blocking the entrance—
"Enter this irregular triangle opening

at your own risk," it seems to say, well,
let's see—fault lines on the concave side
of the larger rock, a mulch-like floor

with small hassock rocks we can
sit on—even today, and look up
through the cluster of dead leaves

partially blocking the eye-shaped
opening at the apex, look up past
the sheer grey sides of what seems

to be dead rock at bristles of green
leaves brushing blue sky . . . later,
standing atop the pitched rock tent,

I can see red stains in the shape of
a cross above the thin crack of eye
with a black hole pupil—mysterious

red stains—no natural causes that
I can see . . . seems as good a place
to die as any, I think, looking down

through what is now a faint smile
shaped crack where the two rocks
meet at what could be, what will be,

"what is," the increasingly familiar old
rasping voice of cold wind whispers
insistently, "what is, not what could be,

what is." O.K., Abram, if you say so,
what is your place of final unrest.

Wharf Road

an irregular diagonal from Dogtown Square
to the Commons Road, it "is especially
notable . . . for its borders of blueberry
and huckleberry bushes, whose deep purple

"foliage in the autumn is set off, here and
there, by bright yellow witch-hazel leaves.
Along this road, too, are some of the most
picturesque cedars in Dogtown." (C&R, p.39)

Let's pause here in the shade of the cedars,
near the remains of an old well, near the stone
with the number 24 carved and painted black,
the same black we have seen ere this.

Let's pause near the stone marking the spot
that was once the residence of Abram Wharf,
one of the sturdy villagers; yes, my friend,
pause here, right here, right now, even though

we hear so clear his old raspy voice saying,
"No, no, go, just go!" Right now, we'll pause,
rest, and drink from the old well as deeply
as we can, and share some berries, juicy

and sweet, huckle and blue—handful after
handful of pure nourishment we offer to
any tormented, wandering spirit who
may be in the area—including Abram,

of course, and you, dear reader,
dear friend, including you.

"No Thanks,"

Abram's raspy voice whispers fiercely,
"What would I do with your berries—
you can stuff them where the sun
don't shine—that's not the food

"I need—as you well know—I need
something that will lessen the grief
that cannot be lessened, the grief
that becomes worse every year—

"that (I fear) will keep accumulating
til eternity—now will you cease
meddling—take your notebook, your
camera, your goody two-shoes mind

"and leave, please leave me to deal with
my guilt and my tormentors alone!"

Old Abram's Last Words

"And oh, one last thing
you should know before you go—

"I'd do it again!"

Thomasine (Tammy) Younger—Continued

the geezer understan's how someone can feel a strange mixture
of pain and comfort—the feelin's I get from bein' trapped here
with that ol' fart, the sneerin' righteous Abram, supposed to be
so educated, but really dum'—his head as addled by superstishin'
as the rest a them—he really believed, still believes it was

my spells killed his sheep—when they died from neglect—
an tryin' ta eat stones—he was too busy pokin' his nose into
other people's business . . .
        ol' neighbor Wharf so proud of
his f...in' cousin, the judge (how many witches did he condemn—
I wonder) . . .
        the same strange mixture I get from bein' with
that wise-arse clown, that would-never-be artist, that man of
many names, that "captain," who couldn't row across Folly Cove
without getting seasick,—"esteemed man of the community"
one guy said in one o' them books—esteemed, my arse,
the only one who ever esteemed him was hisself—Ahh!
the pain of being bound with that would-be dentist
fer the last two hundred years—livin' and relivin'
that Sunday afternoon—his taunt, "your teeth are just
like you," he said, with his f...in' smirk, "too onery
to do anythin' with them," his words still ringin'
in my ears, still echoin' through the years—Oh! Oh!
My mouth still hurts whenever I think of him—that
sonovabitch—
        an' the comfort of hatin', of wishin'
I really had some witch powers—that f...er would of
been clutchin' his gut every minute of every day
of the last couple a centuries and beyond—mebbe

I aint got them kinda powers—but I know he knows
what I thinks of him—wishes count for somethin'—
all our spiteful wishes count—his, mine, ol' Abram's—
they bind us together—fact is we're all stuck here
in this terminal moraine—feelin' the same comfort,
the same pain, I 'magine. . . .
                                    Ol' Abram, of course
he's feelin' pain—noone can kill hisself and feel good
about it—him I understand, but f...in' would-be-Captain
Jack—what's keepin' him here? Could it be me?
mebbe, but theres somethin' between him and Abram—
somethin' more serious than the pain of rotting teeth
pulled halfway out. . . .

Oh, I hope they're both clutchin' their gut!
Or worse! Like me, livin' and relivin' a pathetic
useless life . . . kinda sad when you think bout it . . .
the three of us, each tried by each other, found guilty
and sentenced to be tied to each other and to these
accursed rocks by countless threads of spite and thought . . .

oh! the ol geezer don't like that—resentment, bitterness,
spite, and self pity, evil, all evil, he says, that eats away
at the soul, the trinity of Abram, Captain Jack, and you,
he says, all have to get over it—
                                    get over it! Pugh! easy
for him to say—he hasn't had the words of those two arseholes
and all the other self-righteous villagers ringin' in his ears
for the last two centuries . . .

Black Neil (Cornelius Finson)

A freed slave, a clerk for the boat fishers
of 'Squam, and hog butcher for local inhabitants,

his teeth, one old lady insisted, were
"fully an inch in length." (Mann, p.25) "He was

"firmly persuaded that when Molly Jacobs died
she left buried treasure in her cellar, and it was
with difficulty he could be kept away
from the quite uninhabitable hole."

Long after Judy Rhines had left for Boston,
"he lingered around her house, until its walls
fell in, when he sought refuge in the cellar."

Neil was "cold, dirty, half-starved, and shaking
with the combined infirmity of old age and fright . . .
[when] on a bitter day in winter, 1830 [he was taken
from this cellar hole] by Constable William Tucker
of Riverdale—the people of that village having
complained of the case to the Overseers of the Poor—
and carried off to the almshouse."

After the Constable and Neil left a store where
they stopped to get warm, a man, Mark Allen, said,
"There, I'll bet he'll be so comfortable
at the poor house that he won't live a week." (Mann, p.51)

Comfortable or not—within seven days,
Neil was dead.

Judy Rhines (1771–1833+)

niece of Tammy Younger, lived on the Commons Road,
just below where the brook flows over the road.

"Judy was a tall, rawboned woman who had been born
in Sandy Bay in 1771. She made a precarious living,
as several other Dogtown dames did, by going out
occasionally for housework, picking blueberries, and
telling fortunes, and by other unrecorded means.

"She is reputed to have had great courage,
which was so respected that no intruder
dared approach nearer to her house
after she bade him to stop.
                              "Judy Rhines . . .
is said to have had many friends. We judge
that those friends were attracted to her
not by pity, but by her heartiness,
her broad compassion, and perhaps by
a freedom from conventional restraints." (C&R, p.41)

Judy Rhines, Molly Jacobs, and Liz Tucker—
"These three unfortunates comprised
Dogtown's red-light district." (Dresser, p.18)

Thus, new meaning to the name Dogtown—
Think of "dog" as in "You ain't nothin'
but a hound dog" or as in Fats Domino's
"Baby, don't you let your dog bite me."

Interesting that Judy is the heroine
of both an old poem by Percy MacKaye
in which she defies and defeats her evil aunt
Tammy and marries the minister's son, and

Diamant's recent novel in which she has
a touching love affair with Black Neil . . .
I'd make her a heroine too . . . if I could.

Old Ruth

"a freed mulatto slave with a hearty,
compassionate manner"—(Dresser, p.16)

she lived for some years on the upper floor
of Esther Carter's house and climbed
by outside stairs to her lodging—a ledge
just beyond that slight depression that
was once a cellar hole—a ledge is named
after her—
        "She also was known as ['Tia'
or] 'John Woodman.' She usually was employed
for building stone walls and other heavy
outdoor work to which she had become
accustomed when she was young." (C&R, p.36)

She was "of a happy spirit, kind-hearted and
religious; her voice could be heard singing hearty
gospel songs as her big muscled arms would lift
and move the huge stones into place. . . . Her
physical strength reflected a kind of spiritual
power that made her a symbol of dependability." (Higgins, p.20)

"Since she did a man's work, she dressed
accordingly. It was only when she went
to the poorhouse to spend her last days
that she began to wear a skirt, and that was
by compulsion, not by her choice." (C&R, p.36)

Sad, so sad, the compulsive ways
in which we spend our last days.

Ruth's Ledge

"as you recede farther from the . . . ocean and approach Gloucester,
you come [upon] still wilder ledges, unsafe without a guide"
(Higginson, p.254)

not really ledge—just a grout pile, rejected boulders,
rocks, left for dead by a glacier, no other reason
for this formation on this forsaken hilltop, miles
from the sea—so dead it appears that even the green
fern skirts on the nearest can't give them life—

they are not climbing out of the shade of red cedars,
nor crawling up over the others, neither Darwin,
nor the Druids, not even halfway intelligent design
could explain this—
      these stones, neither good
nor evil, neither the fit nor the unfit crowning
the top of the pile—sunlight glinting alike on all
the odd shapes, on "all the rocks not needed
in the rest of the earth" (Garland, p.58) on all
the rocks that fell as they happened to fall. . . .

Imagine two hundred years ago, Old Ruth (a.k.a.
John Woodman) after a hard day of lifting boulders
into stone walls, sitting here in her dungarees,
humming her gospel songs, resting and staring out
at the lengthening shadows of the stones as the night
breeze brushes her close-cropped hair. . . .
        Imagine
Ruth, oblivious of the insects, sitting atop this jumble
of rock—white moonlight glancing off the whole

misbegotten collection of sharp and blunt, large
and small arrowheads pointing everywhere and
nowhere—to everyone and no one—to present
and past, male and female, would-be poet and
gospel singer, professor and professional builder
of stone walls, thinking how beautiful
these rocks are, lying here, just the way
they happened to fall. . . .
                              Oh! Whoa!
Look at that—two cracks in the topmost stone—
No, No! It can't be—not a winking eye,
definitely not—the faint hint of a smile.

John Morgan Stanwood (1774–1852)

(Johnny Morgan, Morgan Stanwood, Granther Stannard,
Captain Jack, Captain Morgan, et al.) "not aliases
but . . . terms used by friendly neighbors when referring to
a thoroughly estimable member of the community." (C&R, p.42)

"Morgan Stanwood never went to the wars,
so those who knew him as Capt. . . . made a mistake
if they thought the title a military one." (Mann, p.63)
Maybe a sea captain—who went on foreign voyages,
but returned to marry Mary Lurvey and have many children.

In his later years he became the village cobbler.
"At first he did his cobbling in a little shed
attached to [his] house, but he had a large number
of children, and as they grew up, they and their callers
caused so much confusion around the house
that the old gentleman built a hut near a big rock
by the side of the road, where he could cobble
in peace.
                "The hut [his 'boo'] was made of slabs
and covered with turf, and the hole in the bank
where it stood is still clearly visible." (C&R, p.42)

"On a shelf in the corner [of his boo] he kept a book
in which he made a record of . . . interesting matters." (Mann, p.64)

Before he became convinced his legs were made
of glass, (Mann, p.25) he practiced itinerant dentistry.
"On one occasion Tammy Younger sent for him
to extract from her upper jaw two rather large teeth
which had become painful. [He] pulled each tooth
part way out and . . . left . . . them dangling there for a time,

"telling Tammy that her teeth were so obstinate that he could
do nothing more with them." (C&R, p.42)

At the Boo

Took some trouble to find it but here it is—
the slight indentation in the bank, growing
slighter and slighter every year, no slabs,
no turf, just a few oak leaves scattered here

in the old boo where John Morgan Stanwood
kept his record of interesting matters, not much
to look at, but when I become quiet and sit still
and solitary, the past offers itself up, the spirit

of Captain Jack, himself, swirls the oak leaves,
"Pick them up," his silky voice makes me an offer
I cannot refuse, "Read the messages," it says,
and when I pick up the dead leaves, turn them

over in my palm . . . O miracle of miracles—
I can read the hieroglyphics
of dried and brittle veins.

Fragments from the Book John Morgan Stanwood Kept in the Corner of his Boo

July 28, 1814

. . . had a talk with ol' Abram today—
I almost felt sorry for him—a sad spectacle, so ol'
an' feeble, so depressed—feelin' evil in the place, he said,
silly fool, still blamin' ugly ol' Tammy for his dead sheep,—
kinda strange, I tol' him, you believing in witchcraft,
even though you don't believe in your religion—
not any more than I do . . .

August 3, 1814

. . . Ol' Abram again, and him still complainin'
'bout how much trouble it was to get thru the day—
why bother, I tol' him, like I tol' him so many times afore,
why bother, if I was you with nothin' left from your grand farm
'cept one lonely pig, a couple a cows—an a house that's
fallin' to ruin around you, and black Neil and Judy Rhines
your closest neighbors . . .
                                    It's not as if your life could
possibly get any better—I tol' him—it's only gonna get worse
and worst—like I said afore,
I almost felt sorry for him.

August 7, 1814

my fortieth birthday is come and gone—halfway to my grave—
not that any of my sprawlin', squallin' brood knows or

gives a damn . . . well, looks like ol' Abram took my advice—
didn't think he had the gumption, but he did it—killed hisself,

slit his throat with an ol' razor—so now ol' Abram Wharf
is dead, stern, ol' Abram who strutted around on account a
his cousin bein' a judge—so uppity, so judgmental hisself,
so sure he was a good man leadin' a good life—and so proud

of his schoolin'—what good did all that learnin' do him—
Abram Wharf—all he did was live and die here among
these boulders with the rest of us—nice contrast tho,
dontcha think—my birthday, his suicide, life and death
and all that . . . humorless ol' Abram—I wonder,
will he ever get the joke?

Fragments From the Book (continued)

. . . 1821

Well, just back from practicin' some dentistry
on ugly ol' Tammy—funny thing happened when
I was pullin' out her teeth—I got to thinkin' 'bout

how mean and hateful she was, 'bout all the damage
she done to everyone around her, how the whole village
was livin' under a black cloud cause she was livin' in it—

an I had a vision. I 'magined what eternity would
be like with someone like that livin' and hatin' in it,
a fearsome thought—that would be hell, indeed . . .

Well, I thought—if she is gonna live forever, she
should hafta live with her two buck teeth pulled
halfway out for every minute of every hour of

every day of every year . . . I thought—
let me play judge—let that be my sentence.

September 8, 1824

Saw ol' Abram's ghost again
today—no rest, he says,

no rest—in death—no rest
for me, no rest for you,

my kind counselor, my
companion for years and

years to come . . . whoa! whoa!
what a terrifying thought—

that couldn't be true—
could it?

Last Fragments—Undated

. . . I tried to get away—moved
to Gloucester—but no matter
where or when I died—

I find myself here, staked out
with my two most detested souls
on this stingin' hill of reddish rock . . .

. . . death, by the way—death
not that different—same pain—
just a slight distortion—

like lookin' through the prism
of my left leg . . .

Molly Jacobs and Sarah Phipps (aka Sally Jacobs)

Molly and Sarah, two girls who in their youth
"may have given their end of town a swinging
reputation," Garland says, "but if they hastened its
decline, they at least broke the cheerlessness of it." (p.63)

Grown up, grown old, they would while away
their time, playing cards. "Sarah would get mad
at Molly, and say: 'I shan't tell you where I hid
the kerds. I hid them behind the old chest,
but I shan't tell you.'" (Mann, p.55)

Grown up, grown old, having played
the hand they were dealt—they lay together
(Molly and Sally Jacobs) in tattered rags
pulled up over their chins—they lay together

in their bed through the cold winter
days and nights—the snow fallen and
falling through what was once a roof—
lying there in each others' arms—

barely moving, only slightly disturbing
the smooth white blanket
that covered them.

Thomasine (Tammy) Younger—Continued

the villagers is so hare-brained, so pathetic, such
f...in' arseholes—but mebbe I should be thankful—
their ignorance was my livelihood—some moldy bread
here, some firewood there, a stinkin' fish or two—if
I was lucky—all I had to do was open my wooden window
and I would get somethin', some tribute from everyone
who passed my door . . . my power was in their minds—

they were so sure I could transform myself (or them)
into any bird or beast—it was so easy to start the silliest
of stories—like that one of the sore legged crow—I just
walked with a limp for a couple of days an' bout everyone
in Gloucester had seen me flyin' overhead, wounded
from a blast from a shotgun, leg trailin' behind me—

aah, it was so easy, too easy perhaps to become a witch,
to become one of the devil's party without knowin' it—
I'd feel (still feel) a sharp twinge every now and then—
I know—or part of me does—what I did was wrong—
don't mistake me now—I don't regret for one second
wringin' what meager tribute I could out of those half-wit
villagers. . . .
          The ol' geezer understan's what I is talkin' 'bout,
what gnaws at me is I knows, deep inside I knows I helped
keep belief in witchcraft alive—I knows 'bout all the women
who have been, will be beaten, tortured, and killed by
ignorant, self-righteous snobs and mobs—
                                        I hafta admit

he's right! At least some of the blood of many innocents
is on my hands—but what choice did I have—short, wizened
and overweight—ugly old cow of a woman—even when I
was young—I couldn't sell myself, no one would buy . . .

not like my niece Judy and her friends who gave "Dogtown"
its name—who turned our rock-strewn never-would-be farms
into Gloucester's red light district—Rhines, Jacobs, Phipps,
and Tucker—the f...ers—hafta laugh tho, when I think of
the damned fools that would come to visit them one day,
then preach against them the next—Aarrggh!—f...in'
hypocrites—nothing I hates more than f...in' hypocrites. . . .

And where is their youth now, where are those bodies,
those well-rounded bodies—well worn from overuse, worn
nearly as smooth as the rocks around us? Gone! bodies
all gone—bodies old and bodies sold—long gone—
didn't, don't last more than a few years. . . . Aaah! the body—

don't miss it that much . . . 'cept when I thinks bout the waste,
bout Molly and Sally lying together 'neath their white sheets,
thinks mebbe I shoulda been born a couple hundred years later,
mebbe then I wouldn't be so hateful an bitter—wha's that
the geezers sayin', they've got a word for it now—repression—
nothing makes you as bitter and as hateful as repression . . .
hmmm, hmmm . . . mebbe the geezer
does understand some things . . . hmmm, hmmm . . .

Sammy Stanley

"whose real name was Sam Maskey,
took care of the old women [Molly Jacobs
and Sarah Phipps aka Sally Jacobs] until
they were removed to the poorhouse. . . .

"Although Sammy wore men's trousers,
he had been brought up by his grandmother
as though he were a girl, and wherever he went
he wore a handkerchief tied over his head."

His grandmother kept him busy at housework—
until she went to the almshouse, and "he was left
to shift for himself, he moved to Sandy Bay
and earned a livelihood there by going out

"to work for his neighbors as a 'washerwoman.'
Despite his attire and his domestic occupation,
however, Sammy had sufficient innate shrewdness . . .
to save enough money from his earnings . . . to become

"a stockholder in the cotton mill
that was established there." (C&R, p.40)

Marsden Hartley (1877–1943)

"The products of his singular, mystical . . . encounter
[with the Dogtown landscape] were the pivot
upon which his later career turned."—(O'Gorman, p.21)

"Dogtown is mine." Marsden Hartley (quoted by O'Gorman, p.16)

The Old Bars, Dogtown, 1936
Oil on composition board, (Cape Ann Museum, p.20)

Wedged between and sticking up
out of the signature boulders piled
atop one another at the back

of a clearing with a glinting rock
head surfacing out of a green sea
in the center—the old bars, in light

and shadow, blunter, larger than
life—in a rough circle, Dogtown's
grotesque Stonehenge, pointing

everywhichway at all kinds of odd
angles into the blue with three
sour cream pancake clouds—burnt

brown in the center—clouds that
turn unexpectedly into three alien
spacecraft, then into three off-white

ghosts hovering over the remains—
and finally into empty cartoon bubbles
in which Hartley refused to put

the old bars' thoughts; we have
to supply our own captions.

Dogtown, the Last of the Stone Wall, c. 1934
Oil on academy board, (Cape Ann Museum, p.24)

Ugly vegetation poking up its stubby fingers
testing the prevailing winds—or tusks of
a brown boar trying to impale the swishy

fish clouds swimming in a blue sky sea—
the last of the stone wall is in the center
of the painting—bleached grey-white bones

(femur, tibia, fibia, et al.) lie where they fell
beneath what could be, what should be
an empty hollow skull—
                                            from the skyline,
toward the left margin, thin ethereal figures
(ghosts of past and present) survey the scene.

Note Hartley's initials, in black on one
of the foundation bone-stones.

News (June 25, 1984)

Anne Natti, a teacher who specialized
in teaching students with dyslexia,

was murdered by Peter Hodgkins—
who crushed her skull with one

of the smaller Dogtown boulders. See
Elyssa East's *Dogtown: Death and Enchantment*

in a New England Ghost Town
for as close to the full story

as we are likely to get.

Peter Hodgkins' Letter Written from Jail to Elyssa East

"Something calls to me. The trees are calling me near,
I have to find out why. The gentle Voices I hear . . .
Draw me to going to the woods . . . I would hear the Elders
of the trees speaking to me Strange but that is how
I connect myself with the woods. One has to beleave[sic]
in the Forces." (East, p.249)

Re: the veracity of Peter's letters—
East says, "I [am] not so confident. . . . They left me with
an impression of a man who is extremely eager to please.

"Hodgkins tells me what he thinks I want to hear, then
immediately says or does nearly the opposite. . . . He seems
to be truly, deeply confused." (East, p.249)

Welcome Peter!
Welcome Elyssa! Welcome everyone
to the Dogtown wobble.

Searching for the Site

The murder site—can't find it, too many
side trails leading nowhere—I guess
this small clearing I've never seen before

will be as good as any to rest and think
about Hodgkins and his voices—the elders
of the trees he heard speaking to him—

can't imagine any of my trinity
of misbegotten souls tempting him
to take that teacher's life—they've

got enough to deal with already—
"You got that right, at least," all three
of the by now familiar voices insist in

eerie harmony, "Nice to see you agree
on something," I say, then wall them out,
and sit here quiet, still and solitary—

thinking about the voices that tempt us
to murder and create—that whisper
so softly to our inner ear—the voices

that tell us only what we long to hear.

Thomasine (Tammy) Younger—Conclusion

My funeral—ahh! My death, my funeral—I remember
that harebrain Hodgkins, the cabinet maker (whose relative
killed that teacher-girl a few years back)—his family was
spooked so bad, so afeard of me, he moved my casket out
of the house and into a shed in a drivin' rain . . . and Ahh!

My burial, my awe inspirin' burial is still remembered—
people then and now still say I haven't died—how many
villagers can have that said about them—Jesus, and who else? . . .

And the funny thing is that they're right (about that at least)
I'm still here—sellin' the spirit, it appears, is serious,
more serious than the mere sellin' of the body, looks like
I'll be here for a spell. . . .
                              O looka there, the old geezer,
writin' again, jotting down something in his notebook—still
harpin' on bitterness, self pity an' spite bein' a dead end!

Wait, wait, wha's that he's sayin'? If I could only bring
myself to wish them well, the spell would break and
we'd all be free—impossible—how can he think I'll ever
wish them well, forgive their trespasses? not likely, tho
it looks like he has—hmmm, hmmm! mine too!

He's forgiven mine too!!! Hmmm! Well, mebbe someday
I'll think about it—if and when they forgive mine, Hmmmm
mebbe we should all think about it . . . Hmmmmm, mebbe,

I is gettin' soft—beginnin' to think about thinkin' kindly
of others—mebbe, as I said afore—it's gettin' close
to closin' time—

　　　　　　mebbe, . . . mebbe not.

Bibliography

Babson, J.J. *History of the Town of Gloucester.* Gloucester MA: Anniversary Edition, Peter Smith, 1972. Large tome on history of Gloucester, a few pages on Dogtown with some information on Wharf's suicide and Revolutionary War widows.

Babson, Roger. "Address before the Gloucester Rotary Club." Gloucester MA: Leo A. Chisholm, September 1927. Dogtown folder, Sandy Bay Historical Society. Compassion for and insight into "tragic" lives of Dogtown residents, the decline "due primarily to economic causes."

Babson, Roger, and Saville, Foster H. *Cape Ann Tourist's Guide.* Gloucester MA: Cape Ann Community League, 1952. Includes useful information concerning location of the cellar holes of the old inhabitants of Dogtown.

Blessington, Francis. *The Last Witch of Dogtown.* Gloucester MA: Curious Traveller Press, 2001. A novel well grounded in Dogtown lore. John Morgan Stanwood is the central character and the witchery of Dogtown all too real.

Cape Ann Museum. *Marsden Hartley: Soliloquy in Dogtown.* Gloucester MA: Cape Ann Museum, 2012. Catalog for the 2012 Hartley exhibit, includes excellent essays by Martha Oaks, James F. O'Gorman, and Peter Anastas.

Carlotto, Mark. *The Cellars Speak.* Create Space Independent Publishers, 2015. Examines the social structure of Dogtown using a data fusion approach that combines maps, genealogy, and oral history.

Carlotto, Mark. *The Dogtown Guide*. Lulu Press, 2008, 2017; Kindle, 2016. A pocket guide to Dogtown, the remains of an abandoned colonial settlement on Cape Ann Massachusetts.

Carlotto, Mark. *The Island Woods*. Create Space Independent Publishers, 2012, 2017. A spatial history of the uninhabited woods of Cape Ann constructed from historical photographs, maps, GPS data, and satellite imagery. Includes accurate maps and good comparative photos of Dogtown, past and present.

Carlsen, Carl, Ed. *The Poetry of Places in Essex County*. Danvers MA: North Shore Community College, 2013. http://www.poetryofplaces. org. History, photographs and lots of poetry about Dogtown.

Copeland, Melvin T., and Rogers, Elliott C. *The Saga of Cape Ann*. Freeport ME: The Bond Wheelwright Company, 1960. Dogtown chapter recounts, crystallizes Mann's stories, a helpful, easy to read summary.

Diamant, Anita. *The Last Days of Dogtown*. New York: Scribner, 2005. This novel is an intelligent, sensitive treatment of the old Dogtowners by the author of *The Red Tent*. She adds her own salt and pepper to the old Dogtown stories, especially to the relationship between Judy Rhines and Cornelius Finson.

Dresser, Thomas. *Dogtown, A Village Lost in Time*. Franconia NH: Thorn Books, 2001. Small trustworthy chapbook with much useful material, including historical detail, thumbnail sketches of the key Dogtown inhabitants, and information on Roger Babson and his boulder trail.

East, Elyssa. *Dogtown: Death and Enchantment in a New England Ghost Town*. New York: Free Press, 2009. A work of narrative non-fiction which succeeds in telling the story of a landscape. It focuses on the murder of Anne Natti in 1984 and has a lot of eerie, authentic detail, plus an excellent chapter on Charles Olson.

Garland, Joseph E. *The Gloucester Guide: A Retrospective Ramble.* Gloucester MA: Gloucester's 350th Anniversary Celebration, Inc., 1973. Important chapter on Dogtown that is organized as a walk through. It has the same old anecdotes about the settlers, but it is written with a poetic sensibility.

Groom, George. Unpublished Typescript. Dogtown folder, Sandy Bay Historical Society. Useful comments on some of the old settlers.

Higgins, Paul Lambourne. *Moon Over Cape Ann*. Rockport MA: Rockport Colony, 1978. Perceptive chapbook, with helpful, well-written comments on Tammy Younger, Judy Rhines, and Old Ruth and some common sense criticism of Percy MacKaye's poem.

Higginson, Thomas Wentworth. *Oldport Days*. Boston MA: Lee and Shepard, 1888. Reveals a touch of the poet in his treatment of the "druidic" boulders of Dogtown Common.

MacKaye, Percy. *Dogtown Common*. New York: Macmillan, 1921. Long poem in which the heroine, Judy Rhines, defeats her evil aunt Tammy and marries the minister's son.

Mann, Charles. *The Story of Dogtown*. Gloucester MA: Procter Brothers, 1896. The basic treasury of Dogtown lore, much of which is collected from interviews of local inhabitants. Some stories a bit far-fetched.

Naismith, Helen. *Walking Cape Ann with Ted Tarr*. Gloucester MA: Ten Pound Island Book Co., 1994. Contains 30 pages on Dogtown, in which she retraces her walks with Ted Tarr. It also contains 10 pages of accurate maps which could be helpful for anyone planning walks through the Dogtown landscape.

Oaks, Martha. "Turn Yr Back on the Sea, go inland, to Dogtown." Catalog for the Marsden Hartley exhibit, Gloucester MA: Cape Ann Museum, 2012, pp.5-13. A perceptive, intelligent essay on Marsden Hartley's relationship to Dogtown.

O'Gorman, James F. "Marsden Hartley: 'The' Painter of Dogtown." Catalog for the Marsden Hartley exhibit, Gloucester MA: Cape Ann Museum, 2012, pp.15-22. An art critic's perspective on Hartley's Dogtown paintings.

Olson, Charles. *The Maximus Poems*, Ed. George F. Butterick. Berkeley CA: University of California Press, 1983. Major work of a well-known modern American poet which includes his unique take on Dogtown.

Parsons, Kitty. *Dogtown Common*. Self published, 1936. Rhymed poem with stanzas on many of the old Dogtowners.

Pope, Eleanor. *The Wilds of Cape Ann*. Boston MA: Nimrod, 1981. Dogtown chapter includes three guided walks through the Dogtown terrain and some valuable information on the flora and fauna of the region.

Pringle, James R. *History of Gloucester*. Gloucester MA: Ten Pound Island Book Co., 1997. Not that much on Dogtown, but some relevant comments on the decline of the village.

Sucholeiki, Irving. *A Return to Dogtown: A Look at the Artifacts Left Behind by Some of Cape Ann's Early Settlers*. Gloucester MA: Chisholm and Hunt Printers, 1992. Small book that is what its title says. It focuses on three cellar holes ("unknown," Granny Day, and Abram Wharf), some genealogical material on Day and Wharf families.

Swan, Marshall, W. S. *Town on Sandy Bay*. Canaan NH: Phoenix Publishing, 1980. Not much on Dogtown, except a Faustian legend comment.

Thoreau, Henry David. *The Journal, Vol. VIII-XIV, Nov. 1855-1861*, Eds. Torrey and Allen. New York: Dover Publishing, 1962. Thoreau's comments on Dogtown are incisive and poetic.

About the Author

James R. Scrimgeour received his BA from Clark University, his MA and PhD from the University of Massachusetts, Amherst and is Professor Emeritus at Western Connecticut State University. He has served as Editor of *Connecticut Review* and has published nine books of poetry and over 220 poems in anthologies and periodicals. He has been nominated for several Pushcart Prizes and has given over 250 public readings of his work, including one at an International Conference on Poetry and History, Stirling, Scotland. He has been invited to participate in NEH Seminars on Modern Poetry at NYU and Princeton and has recently served on panels at the Massachusetts Poetry Festival. He was one of five Connecticut poets featured on a CBS poetry blog and is now Poet Laureate of New Milford, CT. He currently conducts poetry programs in libraries, both in New Milford and in Rockport, MA, where he and his wife, Christine Xanthakos Scrimgeour, spend much of their time.

Also by James R. Scrimgeour

Poetry Books

Balloons Over Stockholm
Brushstrokes of the Millennium
We Are What We Have Loved
The Route and Other Poems
Dikel, Your Hands and Other Poems

Chapbooks

On Thacher Island
Entangled Landscapes, with J.P. Briggs
Monet in the 20th Century
James R. Scrimgeour: Greatest Hits 1970-2000

Critical Biography

Sean O'Casey

Charity Statement

A portion of the profits from this book will be donated to the Friends of Dogtown. The Friends of Dogtown has been established to conserve, interpret, and celebrate Dogtown's unique historical and ecological heritage for the benefit of the citizens of Cape Ann and the general public.

The Friends of Dogtown is currently a program of Essex County Greenbelt Association, 82 Eastern Avenue, Essex, MA 01929 (ecga@ecga.org), and gifts to the Friends are fully deductible under Greenbelt's charitable status. Donations need to be made payable to Essex County Greenbelt, with a note that they are intended for Friends of Dogtown.